CONTENTS

FOOTBALL PREGAME

A pass with a perfect spiral. A sack that brings momentum to the defense. A kick return that gives great field position to the offense. A block by an offensive lineman that paves the way for an outstanding run by a running back. Those are just some of the reasons why boys and girls and men and women play the great sport of football.

No matter how big or small, there's a place for you on a football team. All you need to do is develop your skills in order to make an impact on the field.

Players enjoy the game of football because of the teamwork that is necessary in order to have success. Skills alone will not make the game fun for anyone. Players on both teams must make sportsmanship a priority in order to enjoy football.

Finally, the tips and drills offered in this book are provided with safety as the top priority. Always practice with full equipment, and do so with an adult or coach nearby in case of an injury. Most of all, have fun!